YOU
HAD
BETTER
MAKE
SOME
NOISE

WORDS MEAN
SOMETHING
DIFFERENT
DEPENDING ON
THE PERSON
WHO SAYS THEM
RIGHT?

GLORIA STEINEM

"IN A GENTLE WAY, YOU CAN SHAKE THE WORLD."

These inspiring words, printed on T-shirts and mugs and engraved on jewelry, are widely attributed to Mahatma Gandhi, legendary social activist and leader of the Indian independence movement. And yet there's no evidence that he ever said or wrote them. Like many of Gandhi's quotations, the words were probably distilled from his writings or speeches.

This isn't surprising. Quotes are chronically paraphrased, misattributed, or made up entirely, and once launched into the world, they take on a life of their own. "To err, as someone said, is human—especially on social media," writes Jacey Fortin in the *New York Times*. "Verification often falls by the wayside when quotations are neatly packaged into inspirational memes or shareable

OTHER PEOPLE'S
WORDS ARE
THE BRIDGE YOU
USE TO CROSS
FROM WHERE
YOU WERE
TO WHEREVER
YOU'RE GOING

ZADIE SMITH

image files. Mistaken attributions can be copied and reposted with the click of a button." Great thinkers, it seems, have never been more susceptible to widespread misrepresentation, which poses no small problem for the rest of us: we depend on their words, especially in turbulent times.

This book recognizes both our impulse to look to history for guidance and our driving desire for truth. If we're going to lean on the words of a luminary, accuracy matters. Thankfully, for someone as misquoted as Gandhi, he left behind plenty of inspiring writings, including his newspaper *Young India*, published between 1919 and 1932—its columns filled with his ideas and opinions.

Some of the quotations collected here will be familiar, many more less so. With such a well of history to tap, it seemed important to refresh the reserves from which we tend to draw. Many of the names, too, will be recognizable, while others may be new to

I QUOTE OTHERS ONLY IN ORDER THE BETTER TO EXPRESS MYSELF

MICHEL DE MONTAIGNE

the reader. It is part of the hopeful message of this book that those dedicated to fighting for change can be found everywhere, that we are connected across geography and time by our shared commitment to justice.

You Had Better Make Some Noise brings together the enduring wisdom and urgent advice of citizen activists, artists, writers, politicians, visionaries, and intellectuals—individuals who have contributed to ongoing struggles for progress and freedom. The majority of the quotations are excerpted from memoirs, speeches, letters, interviews, telegrams, and other works, although poetry and fiction also found their way into this compilation. In the back of the book, capsule biographies provide historical context as well as original source information. And the perforated pages invite readers to pull out the quotes—to move them from the interior to the exterior for daily reinforcement. Who knows? Maybe some of the words printed in

THE
WORDS
WE USE
ARE THE
WORLDS
WE LIVE
IN

RICHARD FORD

this volume will take their place on T-shirts and mugs.

It's striking to note that many of the statements written decades, even centuries, ago are just as relevant today. From Augustine to Ai Weiwei, the voices in this collection remind us that the fight for justice is never over. In the words of Nigerian writer Chinua Achebe, "The need for protesting will never end." Dissent is a constant and resistance is a relay race. It's our turn to take the baton.

IN A
REAL
SENSE

WE ARE
WHAT WE
QUOTE

GEOFFREY O'BRIEN

YOU
HAD
BETTER
MAKE
SOME
NOISE

MALCOLM X

AN UNJUST LAW IS NO LAW AT ALL

AUGUSTINE

WE MUST NOT CONFUSE

DISSENT

WITH

DISLOYALTY

EDWARD R. MURROW

THERE CAN BE ONLY ONE

PERMANENT

REVOLUTION

A MORAL ONE

LEO TOLSTOY

THE MOST RADICAL
REVOLUTIONARY
WILL BECOME A
CONSERVATIVE ON
THE DAY AFTER
THE REVOLUTION

HANNAH ARENDT

WE HAVE WAITED TOO LONG FOR POLITICAL JUSTICE

WE REFUSE TO WAIT ANY LONGER

CHRISTABEL PANKHURST

I HAVE BEEN
FORTY YEARS A SLAVE

AND FORTY YEARS FREE

AND WOULD BE HERE
FORTY YEARS MORE

TO HAVE EQUAL
RIGHTS FOR ALL

SOJOURNER TRUTH

THE HOUR CALLS FOR MORAL GRANDEUR AND SPIRITUAL AUDACITY

ABRAHAM JOSHUA HESCHEL

WE ARE ENGAGED
IN A SPIRITUAL WAR

WE ARE
NOT
LIVING IN
NORMAL
TIMES

MAHATMA GANDHI

WE MAY NOT HAVE CHOSEN THE TIME

BUT THE TIME HAS CHOSEN US

JOHN LEWIS

DO GET
ALL ON FIRE
AND BE AS
CROSS AS
YOU PLEASE

SUSAN B. ANTHONY

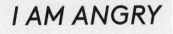

I AM ANGRY

WE SHOULD
ALL BE ANGRY

ANGER HAS
A LONG HISTORY
OF BRINGING
ABOUT POSITIVE
CHANGE

CHIMAMANDA NGOZI ADICHIE

MAYBE YOU CAN'T
OVERRIDE PREJUDICE
OVERNIGHT BUT
THE EMANCIPATION
PROCLAMATION WAS
ISSUED IN 1863

NINETY-ODD
YEARS AGO

I BELIEVE IN
GRADUALISM

I ALSO BELIEVE
THAT NINETY-ODD
YEARS IS PRETTY
GRADUAL

THURGOOD MARSHALL

"WAIT"

HAS ALMOST
ALWAYS MEANT

"NEVER"

MARTIN LUTHER KING JR.

RISES

LIFTING

ROBERT G. INGERSOLL

WE HAVE TO
BE PEOPLE WHO

SET
EACH
OTHER
FREE

HARRY HAY

WE HAVE TO BE PEOPLE WHO SET EACH OTHER FREE — HARRY HAY

MY FAVORITE WORD? IT'S

"ACT"

AI WEIWEI

YOU
WILL NEVER
BE FREE

UNTIL
WE
ARE FREE

DESMOND TUTU

TOLERANCE

IS THE ALPHA
AND OMEGA

OF A NEW
WORLD ORDER

MIKHAIL GORBACHEV

YOU CANNOT UNEDUCATE
THE PERSON WHO HAS
LEARNED TO READ

———

YOU CANNOT HUMILIATE
THE PERSON WHO FEELS PRIDE

———

YOU CANNOT OPPRESS
THE PEOPLE WHO ARE
NOT AFRAID ANYMORE

———

CESAR CHAVEZ

YOU CANNOT OPPRESS THE PEOPLE WHO ARE NOT AFRAID ANYMORE   CESAR CHAVEZ

REACH FOR THE BOOK

IT IS A WEAPON

BERTOLT BRECHT

THERE IS

NO GATE
NO LOCK
NO BOLT

THAT YOU
CAN SET
UPON THE
FREEDOM
OF MY MIND

VIRGINIA WOOLF

CENSORSHIP OF ANY FORM PUNISHES CURIOSITY

SHERMAN ALEXIE

THE MOST

POTENT WEAPON

IN THE HANDS

OF THE OPPRESSOR

IS THE MIND OF

THE OPPRESSED

STEVE BIKO

THE PEOPLE MUST KNOW BEFORE THEY CAN ACT

AND THERE IS NO EDUCATOR TO COMPARE WITH THE PRESS

IDA B. WELLS

THE PURSUIT OF
SCIENTIFIC TRUTH

DETACHED FROM
THE PRACTICAL
INTERESTS OF
EVERYDAY LIFE

OUGHT TO BE
TREATED AS SACRED
BY EVERY
GOVERNMENT

ALBERT EINSTEIN

NOTHING IS MORE RADICAL THAN THE FACTS

MARK BOYLE

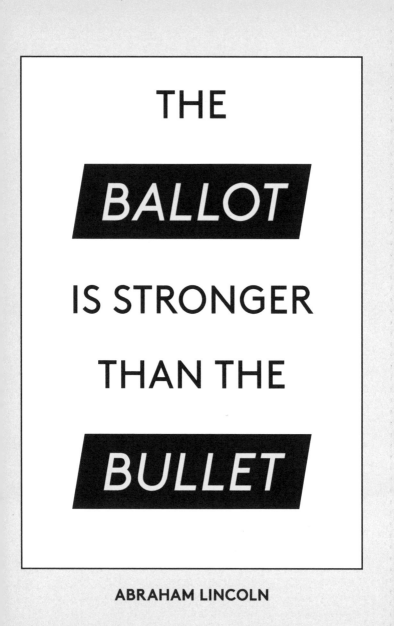

THE

BALLOT

IS STRONGER

THAN THE

BULLET

ABRAHAM LINCOLN

THE MOST
IMPORTANT RULE
FOR AN INDIVIDUAL
IN THIS FIGHT IS
TO FIGURE OUT HOW
NOT TO REMAIN
AN INDIVIDUAL

HOW TO
JOIN A MOVEMENT
BIG ENOUGH TO
CHANGE THE POLITICS

I SHOULD
LIKE TO
BE ABLE TO
LOVE MY
COUNTRY
AND STILL
LOVE JUSTICE

ALBERT CAMUS

WE HAVE TO BEGIN
TO HAVE A
CONVERSATION

THAT
INCORPORATES
A VISION OF LOVE

WITH A VISION
OF OUTRAGE

RUBY SALES

WE NEED POLITICAL MATURITY

WANGARI MAATHAI

WE ARE READY FOR THE DIALOGUE

LECH WAŁĘSA

PEOPLE ALWAYS SAY THAT
I DIDN'T GIVE UP MY SEAT
BECAUSE I WAS TIRED
BUT THAT ISN'T TRUE

NO

THE ONLY TIRED I WAS
WAS TIRED OF GIVING IN

ROSA PARKS

POWER CONCEDES NOTHING WITHOUT A

DEMAND

IT NEVER DID AND IT NEVER WILL

FREDERICK DOUGLASS

WE HAVE TO
TAKE THE BATON
WHEN IT'S
PASSED TO US

AND RUN AS
FAST AND HARD
AS WE CAN

AND THEN
PASS IT ON TO
SOMEONE ELSE

THEODORE SHAW

HISTORY IS A RELAY OF REVOLUTIONS

SAUL ALINSKY

NOT
EVERYTHING
THAT IS
FACED
CAN BE
CHANGED

BUT
NOTHING
CAN BE
CHANGED
UNTIL IT IS
FACED

JAMES BALDWIN

I'VE SEEN
ENOUGH CHANGE
IN MY LIFETIME
TO KNOW
THAT DESPAIR
IS NOT ONLY
SELF-DEFEATING
IT IS UNREALISTIC

SUSAN GRIFFIN

ONLY ACTION CAN ROUSE US

MARGARET MEAD

WE MUST
PUSH *AS*
HARD
AS THEY
PUSH

AND THEN

PUSH
A LITTLE
STRONGER

HARVEY MILK

THERE IS NO TIME
FOR DESPAIR
NO PLACE FOR
SELF-PITY
NO NEED FOR
SILENCE
NO ROOM FOR FEAR

WE SPEAK
WE WRITE
WE DO LANGUAGE

THAT IS HOW
CIVILIZATIONS HEAL

WE ARE THE CHANGE WE SEEK

BARACK OBAMA

REMEMBER TO

RE

ACT

JENNY HOLZER

NOTHING STRENGTHENS
THE JUDGMENT AND QUICKENS
THE CONSCIENCE LIKE
INDIVIDUAL RESPONSIBILITY

ELIZABETH CADY STANTON

SOME ONE OUGHT TO DO IT

SO WHY NOT I?

ANNIE BESANT

I'M SUPPOSED
TO CHRONICLE
WHAT IS SO

AND IT WOULD
BE NICE TO
FORGET HISTORY

BUT WE DO
IT AT OUR PERIL

LUCILLE CLIFTON

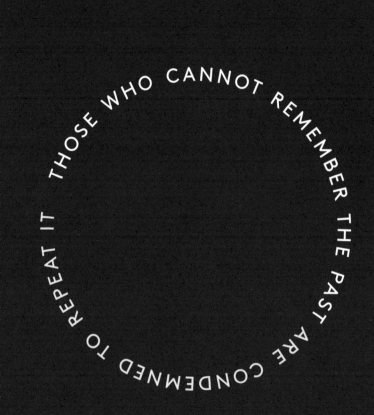

THOSE WHO CANNOT REMEMBER THE PAST ARE CONDEMNED TO REPEAT IT

GEORGE SANTAYANA

KNOWING
WHAT I DO

THERE WOULD
BE NO FUTURE
PEACE FOR ME

IF I KEPT SILENT

RACHEL CARSON

<u>ONCE YOU</u>
<u>FIND THE TRUTH</u>

YOU OUGHT TO
BE PREPARED
TO STAND ON THE
STREET CORNER
AND USE ALL
YOUR GIFTS TO
RIGHT THE WRONG

MAYA ANGELOU

ALWAYS
VOTE

WALT WHITMAN

TO ABSTAIN
FROM
POLITICS IS
IN ITSELF
A POLITICAL
ATTITUDE

SIMONE DE BEAUVOIR

WE NEVER
HAVE DESPAIR
WITHOUT SOME
SMALL HOPE

PIER PAOLO PASOLINI

POLITICS

HATES

A VACUUM

IF IT ISN'T FILLED

WITH HOPE

SOMEONE

WILL FILL IT

WITH FEAR

NAOMI KLEIN

SOMETIMES WE HAVE

TO DO THE WORK

EVEN THOUGH WE DON'T

YET SEE A GLIMMER

ON THE HORIZON THAT

IT'S ACTUALLY GOING

TO BE POSSIBLE

ANGELA DAVIS

HOPE HAS
NEVER
TRICKLED
DOWN

IT HAS
ALWAYS
SPRUNG UP

STUDS TERKEL

THE SIZE OF YOUR DREAMS MUST
ALWAYS EXCEED YOUR CURRENT
CAPACITY TO ACHIEVE THEM

IF YOUR DREAMS DO NOT
SCARE YOU THEY ARE

NOT
BIG

ENOUGH

ELLEN JOHNSON SIRLEAF

REFUSE

TO BE AN ACCOMPLICE

SIMONE WEIL

WE MUST ALWAYS
TAKE SIDES

NEUTRALITY HELPS
THE OPPRESSOR

NEVER
THE VICTIM

ELIE WIESEL

IN REALITY
THERE IS
NO SUCH
THING AS
NOT VOTING

☐ YOU EITHER
VOTE BY VOTING

☐ OR YOU VOTE
BY STAYING HOME
AND TACITLY
DOUBLING THE
VALUE OF SOME
DIEHARD'S VOTE

DAVID FOSTER WALLACE

LIFE

SHRINKS
OR
EXPANDS

IN PROPORTION

TO ONE'S

COURAGE

ANAÏS NIN

YOU CAN'T SPEND
YOUR WHOLE
LIFE CRITICIZING
SOMETHING

AND THEN
WHEN YOU HAVE
THE CHANCE
TO DO IT BETTER
REFUSE TO
GO NEAR IT

VÁCLAV HAVEL

THE ARTIST
MUST TAKE SIDES

PAUL ROBESON

YOUR SILENCE
WILL NOT
PROTECT YOU

AUDRE LORDE

IT IS TIME TO SEE OUR
MORAL CHOICES AS
OUR DESCENDANTS WILL

GEORGE MONBIOT

TO SIN BY
SILENCE
WHEN

WE SHOULD
PROTEST

MAKES
COWARDS
OUT OF MEN

ELLA WHEELER WILCOX

NATURE

IS PARTY TO ALL
OUR DEALS
AND DECISIONS

AND SHE HAS
MORE VOTES

A LONGER MEMORY

AND A STERNER
SENSE OF JUSTICE
THAN WE DO

WENDELL BERRY

I THINK
HAVING LAND AND
NOT RUINING IT

_____

IS THE MOST
BEAUTIFUL ART
THAT ANYBODY
COULD EVER
WANT TO OWN

ANDY WARHOL

ACTION

BRINGS WITH IT
ITS OWN COURAGE

ITS OWN ENERGY

A GROWTH OF
SELF-CONFIDENCE
THAT CAN BE
ACQUIRED IN
NO OTHER WAY

ELEANOR ROOSEVELT

A GROWTH OF SELF-CONFIDENCE THAT CAN BE ACQUIRED IN NO OTHER WAY – ELEANOR ROOSEVELT

FEELING _GOOD_ _IS NOT_ _ENOUGH_

CREATE _A POLITICAL_ _MOMENT_

TANIA BRUGUERA

TO SIN BY
SILENCE
WHEN

WE SHOULD
PROTEST

MAKES
COWARDS
OUT OF MEN

ELLA WHEELER WILCOX

GREAT

<u>PROTESTS</u>

<u>ARE</u>

GREAT

<u>ART</u>

<u>WORKS</u>

SARAH SZE

THE
BEST WAY
TO GET
INSIDE
CITY HALL

IS TO MAKE NOISE ON THE STREET

BHAIRAVI DESAI

IT'S
ALWAYS
TOO
SOON
TO
GO
HOME
AND
IT'S
ALWAYS
TOO
SOON
TO
CALCULATE
EFFECT

REBECCA SOLNIT

REVOLUTIONS

DO NOT

STAND

STILL

ROSA LUXEMBURG

AND LESS DOGMA

CAMILLE PAGLIA

DO NOT WAIT FOR *ME* TO DO SOMETHING FOR YOUR RIGHTS

IT'S YOUR WORLD

AND YOU CAN CHANGE IT

MALALA YOUSAFZAI

MAKING NOISE IS MAKING CHANGE

A VICTORY IS SCORED WHEN YOUR OPPONENTS ARE FORCED TO DEBATE ISSUES THEY WOULD RATHER LEAVE IGNORED

OWEN JONES

EVERY REVOLUTION
WAS FIRST A THOUGHT
IN ONE MAN'S MIND

RALPH WALDO EMERSON

DISSENT REBELLION

AND ALL-AROUND

HELL-RAISING

REMAIN THE

TRUE DUTY OF PATRIOTS

BARBARA EHRENREICH

ON
THIS EARTH
THERE IS
NO HAPPINESS
WITHOUT A
LONGING FOR
JUSTICE

JOHN BERGER

I COULD NOT BE

A POLITICAL ACTIVIST

WITHOUT

A SENSE OF HUMOR

AND WITHOUT

A SENSE OF JOY

MARTÍN ESPADA

THE ROLE
OF THE
ARTIST
IS THAT
OF THE
SOLDIER
OF THE
REVOLUTION

DIEGO RIVERA

WE
ARE
THE
REBELS
ASKING
FOR
THE
STORM

NADYA TOLOKONNIKOVA

JUSTICE
IS LOVE
ON LEGS

SPILLING
OVER
INTO THE
PUBLIC
SPHERE

CORNEL WEST

MAN'S CAPACITY

FOR JUSTICE

MAKES DEMOCRACY

<u>POSSIBLE</u>

BUT MAN'S INCLINATION

TO INJUSTICE

MAKES DEMOCRACY

<u>NECESSARY</u>

REINHOLD NIEBUHR

DISOBEDIENCE

IN THE EYES
OF ANYONE
WHO HAS
READ HISTORY

IS MAN'S
ORIGINAL
VIRTUE

OSCAR WILDE

A LITTLE REBELLION

NOW AND THEN

IS A GOOD THING

THOMAS JEFFERSON

IRREVERENCE IS THE CHAMPION OF LIBERTY

AND
ITS ONLY
SURE
DEFENSE

MARK TWAIN

IT'S WORTH REMEMBERING THIS

FREEDOM
OF
EXPRESSION

SUSTAINS ALL THE OTHER
FREEDOMS WE ENJOY

IAN MCEWAN

ALL MEN RECOGNIZE
THE RIGHT OF REVOLUTION

THAT IS

THE RIGHT TO REFUSE
ALLEGIANCE TO AND TO RESIST
THE GOVERNMENT

WHEN ITS TYRANNY OR
ITS INEFFICIENCY ARE
GREAT AND UNENDURABLE

HENRY DAVID THOREAU

COURAGE

IS AS CONTAGIOUS AS FEAR

SUSAN SONTAG

I CANNOT AND WILL NOT CUT MY CONSCIENCE TO FIT THIS YEAR'S FASHIONS

LILLIAN HELLMAN

DARE THEM TO

CENSOR YOU

KEN LOACH

I AM

INVESTED

IN

ILLUSTRATING

THE

POSSIBLE

THEASTER GATES

MY WISH

USE ART TO TURN THE WORLD INSIDE OUT

JR

HOW IMPORTANT IS ART AS A FORM OF PROTEST?

VERY

JEREMY DELLER

ANOTHER WORLD
IS NOT ONLY POSSIBLE

SHE IS ON HER WAY

ON A QUIET DAY
I CAN HEAR HER
BREATHING

ARUNDHATI ROY

HOPE
DIES
LAST

JESSIE DE LA CRUZ

NEVER MEASURE THE HEIGHT OF A MOUNTAIN

UNTIL YOU HAVE
REACHED THE TOP

THEN YOU WILL SEE
HOW LOW IT WAS

DAG HAMMARSKJÖLD

ONE OF THE
MEANINGS OF
HUMAN EXISTENCE

THE SOURCE OF
HUMAN FREEDOM

IS NEVER TO
ACCEPT ANYTHING
AS DEFINITIVE
UNTOUCHABLE
OBVIOUS OR
IMMOBILE

MICHEL FOUCAULT

CRITICAL
THINKING
WITHOUT
HOPE IS
CYNICISM

HOPE
WITHOUT
CRITICAL
THINKING IS
NAÏVETÉ

MARIA POPOVA

TO ME *THESE* ARE THE GOOD OLD DAYS NOT BECAUSE THEY'RE GOOD

BUT BECAUSE WE ARE ALIVE TO EXPERIENCE AND TO CHANGE THEM

BARBARA KRUGER

THE

REAL
RADICAL

IS THAT PERSON

WHO HAS A VISION OF EQUALITY

AND IS WILLING TO DO THOSE

THINGS THAT WILL BRING REALITY

CLOSER TO THAT

VISION

BAYARD RUSTIN

DO NOT LET US
SPEAK OF
DARKER DAYS
LET US SPEAK
RATHER OF
STERNER DAYS

WINSTON CHURCHILL

EITHER WE ALL LIVE IN A DECENT WORLD

OR
NOBODY
DOES

GEORGE ORWELL

I'M WORKING

TOWARD A WORLD

IN WHICH IT

WOULD BE EASIER

FOR PEOPLE TO

BEHAVE DECENTLY

DOROTHY DAY

ERR IN
THE DIRECTION
OF KINDNESS

GEORGE SAUNDERS

I LAY IN BED
THINKING ABOUT
THE FUTURE

AND HOW
I WOULD LIKE IT TO BE

EVEN IF
I AM NOT THERE

EDDIE MABO

PEOPLE'S

HOPES

GO ON

FOREVER

JUNOT DÍAZ

IT'S A WONDER
I HAVEN'T
ABANDONED
ALL MY IDEALS

THEY SEEM SO
ABSURD AND
IMPRACTICAL

YET I CLING TO
THEM BECAUSE
I STILL BELIEVE

IN SPITE OF
EVERYTHING

THAT PEOPLE
ARE TRULY
GOOD AT HEART

ANNE FRANK

YOU ARE

NEVER

TOO YOUNG

TO LEAD

KOFI ANNAN

THE YOUNG UNDERSTAND THIS SOCIETY

BETTER THAN THEIR
ELDERS THINK
AND BETTER PERHAPS
EVEN THAN THEIR
ELDERS THEMSELVES

CORETTA SCOTT KING

WE ARE AS GREAT
AS OUR BELIEF
IN HUMAN LIBERTY

NO GREATER

AND OUR BELIEF
IN HUMAN LIBERTY
IS ONLY OURS
WHEN IT IS LARGER
THAN OURSELVES

ARCHIBALD MACLEISH

THE TEST OF
A CIVILIZATION IS IN
THE WAY THAT IT
CARES FOR ITS
HELPLESS MEMBERS

PEARL S. BUCK

WE
MUST LOVE
ONE
ANOTHER
OR DIE

W. H. AUDEN

WOMEN

ARE THE

DOOR TO

RECONCILIATION

WITH THE

WORLD

OCTAVIO PAZ

ON THE
WHOLE AND
IN THE
LONG RUN
WE SHALL
GO UP
OR DOWN
TOGETHER

THEODORE ROOSEVELT

IMAGINE
WE ARE
LINKED

NOT
RANKED

GLORIA STEINEM

THE
TRUE DANGER
IS WHEN
LIBERTY IS
NIBBLED AWAY
FOR
EXPEDIENTS
AND
BY PARTS

EDMUND BURKE

LIFE IS NOT
A PROBLEM
IT IS A PROCESS

ONLY CONTINUED
VIGILANCE WILL
ALLOW US TO
HOLD ON TO OUR
OWN FREEDOM

NIKKI GIOVANNI

IN THIS DAY AND AGE
ADVERTISING IS THE WAY
TO SELL THE PRODUCT
AND OUR PRODUCT IS

PEACE

JOHN LENNON

THOSE
WHO MAKE
PEACEFUL
REVOLUTION
IMPOSSIBLE

WILL MAKE
VIOLENT
REVOLUTION
INEVITABLE

JOHN F. KENNEDY

WE ARE HERE
NOT BECAUSE
WE ARE
LAW-BREAKERS

WE ARE HERE
IN OUR EFFORTS
TO BECOME
LAW-MAKERS

EMMELINE PANKHURST

A NEW
WORLD
PRESCRIPTION
MUST BE
WRITTEN
IMMEDIATELY

LARRY KRAMER

FEW WILL HAVE
THE GREATNESS TO
BEND HISTORY ITSELF

BUT EACH OF US
CAN WORK TO
CHANGE A SMALL
PORTION OF EVENTS

AND IN THE TOTAL
OF ALL THOSE ACTS
WILL BE WRITTEN
THE HISTORY OF THIS
GENERATION

ROBERT F. KENNEDY

AND IN THE TOTAL OF ALL THOSE ACTS WILL BE WRITTEN THE HISTORY OF THIS GENERATION.   ROBERT F. KENNEDY

SORRY FOR THE
INCONVENIENCE

WE ARE
TRYING
TO
CHANGE
THE
WORLD

ANONYMOUS

WE
MUST
BE
LISTENED
TO

PRIMO LEVI

NEVER AGAIN IS OBSOLETE <u>NEVER AGAIN IS NOW</u>

ROSE BEAL

WHEN THE
HISTORY OF
OUR TIMES
IS WRITTEN

WILL WE BE
REMEMBERED AS
THE GENERATION
THAT TURNED
OUR BACKS IN
A MOMENT OF
GLOBAL CRISIS

OR WILL IT BE
RECORDED THAT
WE DID THE
RIGHT THING?

NELSON MANDELA

TO ACQUIESCE

IN DESPAIR

IS THE VERY

WAY TO MAKE

DESPAIRING

FORECASTS

COME TRUE

BERTRAND RUSSELL

LET NOT THE DEFEATISTS
TELL US THAT IT IS TOO LATE

IT WILL
NEVER
BE
EARLIER

TOMORROW WILL
BE LATER THAN TODAY

FRANKLIN D. ROOSEVELT

OUR

ORIGINAL

GUIDING

STARS ARE

STRUGGLE

AND HOPE

PABLO NERUDA

IT'S A RESILIENT PLACE
THE WORLD

AND ITS BEAUTY IS STILL
BREATHTAKING

ITS POTENTIAL
STILL ASTONISHING

AND AS FOR THE
MESS WE'VE MADE

YOU CAN CHANGE IT

AND I BELIEVE
YOU'RE GOING TO

SALMAN RUSHDIE

WE HAVE
IT IN
OUR
POWER
TO

BEGIN THE WORLD OVER AGAIN

THOMAS PAINE

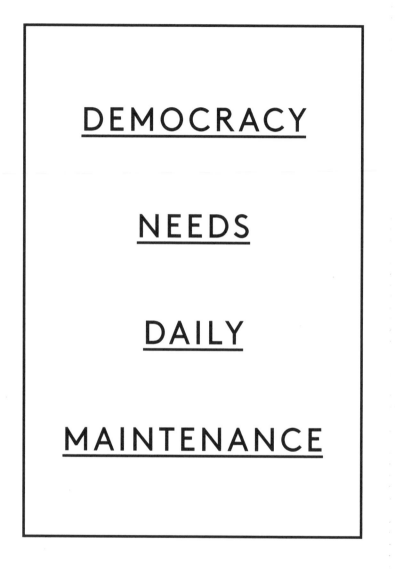

DEMOCRACY

NEEDS

DAILY

MAINTENANCE

SHIRIN EBADI

GIVE ME THE
LIBERTY TO KNOW

TO UTTER AND
TO ARGUE FREELY
ACCORDING TO
CONSCIENCE

ABOVE ALL LIBERTIES

JOHN MILTON

THE NEED FOR PROTESTING WILL NEVER END

CHINUA ACHEBE

BIOGRAPHIES

→ p. 176
CHINUA ACHEBE (1930–2013) was a prolific Nigerian novelist, poet, and critic who published his first and most famous novel, *Things Fall Apart*, in 1958. This line comes from a 1980 interview conducted at the fifth annual conference of the African Literature Association.

→ p. 29
CHIMAMANDA NGOZI ADICHIE (1977–) rose quickly to the top of the literary world with award-winning short fiction and novels, winning a MacArthur "Genius Grant" in 2008. The Nigerian writer has become a powerful advocate for women's rights worldwide, thanks to words such as these from her 2014 book *We Should All Be Feminists*.

→ pp. 34–35
AI WEIWEI (1957–), after studying art in New York City, returned to his native China, where he created work challenging government corruption and repression, leading to his imprisonment and surveillance by the Chinese state. This statement is from a 2009 interview with the curator and critic Hans Ulrich Obrist.

→ p. 41
SHERMAN ALEXIE (1966–), a novelist and poet, won the National Book Award in Young People's Literature for *The Absolutely True Diary of a Part-Time Indian* (2007). These words come from a 2012 interview with *Guernica* magazine.

→ p. 55
SAUL ALINSKY (1909–1972) worked as a community organizer on Chicago's South Side and has influenced generations of activists. These words appear in his 1971 book *Rules for Radicals*, in which he lays out his guiding principles for effecting change through grassroots organizing.

→ p. 71
MAYA ANGELOU (1928–2014), American writer, poet, and activist, is perhaps best known for her 1969 book *I Know Why the Caged Bird Sings*, the first of seven memoirs that experimented with the form of the autobiography. Recipient of a 2010 Presidential Medal of Freedom, Angelou imparted this advice in a 1986 *San Jose Mercury News* interview.

→ p. 148
KOFI ANNAN (1938–), born in Ghana, rose through the ranks to become secretary general of the United Nations in 1997. In 2001 he won the Nobel Peace Prize along with the UN. In his 2015 speech to the One Young World summit, quoted here, he urged youth to take action.

→ p. 28
SUSAN B. ANTHONY (1820–1906) began her activism in the abolitionist movement, but her signal achievement was to pave the way for women's right to vote in the United States. Here, in an 1856 letter, she begs her longtime compatriot Elizabeth Cady Stanton to write a speech for her advocating coeducation.

→ p. 21
HANNAH ARENDT (1906–1975), a Jewish exile from Germany, became one of the leading intellectuals and political theorists of the postwar era. In 1963 she published her famous account of the Adolf Eichmann trial in the *New Yorker*. These words, from an essay titled "Civil Disobedience," appeared in its pages seven years later.

→ p. 152
W. H. AUDEN (1907–1973), born in England, had already cemented his status as one of the greatest British poets of the day before moving to the United States in 1939. His work often carries a political message, as in the poem quoted here, "September 1, 1939," published that year in the *New Republic*.

→ p. 18
AUGUSTINE (354–430) abandoned a career as a professor of rhetoric and found his life's purpose after converting to Christianity. Still regarded as one of the most influential Christian theologians, he left behind a vast array of writings, including these words from *On Free Choice of the Will*.

→ pp. 56–57
JAMES BALDWIN (1924–1987) wrote many acclaimed novels and essays exploring class, race, and sexuality that have become modern classics in American literature. This line comes from "As Much Truth as One Can Bear," a 1962 essay in the *New York Times Book Review* urging writers to wage "guerrilla warfare with . . . American complacency."

→ p. 165
ROSE BEAL (1921–2014) immigrated to the United States from Germany shortly after Kristallnacht on November 9, 1938. She went on to dedicate her life to education and spoke publicly about her experiences in Nazi Germany. This phrase is engraved on the Anne Frank Human Rights Memorial in Boise, Idaho.

→ p. 73
SIMONE DE BEAUVOIR (1908–1986), French author of the feminist classic *The Second Sex* (1949), also wrote novels and, like her companion Jean-Paul Sartre, philosophical works on existentialist themes. This observation comes from her 1960 autobiography, *The Prime of Life*.

→ p. 110
JOHN BERGER (1926–2017), born in England, wrote the 1972 book *Ways of Seeing*, which proposed a revolutionary framework for viewing art based on socially conscious humanism. He was also a champion of human rights, as demonstrated in these words from his essay collection *Hold Everything Dear: Dispatches on Survival and Resistance* (2007).

→ p. 91
WENDELL BERRY (1934–), an award-winning novelist, poet, essayist, activist, and fifth-generation farmer in Kentucky, has been a consistent and passionate advocate for the environment. Here he endorses environmentalist Charles E. Little's 1995 book *The Dying of the Trees*.

→ p. 67
ANNIE BESANT (1847–1933) left an unhappy marriage to become an outspoken champion of many causes in Britain, including access to birth control, workers' rights, and, later, Indian independence. In this line from her 1893 autobiography, she explains her philosophy of action.

→ p. 42
STEVE BIKO (1946–1977) led South Africa's Black Consciousness Movement when he was only in his twenties. His murder while in police custody made him an enduring symbol for the anti-apartheid cause. In this speech delivered at a 1971 student conference, he argued that psychological liberation is necessary in order to achieve racial equality.

→ p. 45
MARK BOYLE (1934–2005), a Scottish artist, became known for his experimental, psychedelic light shows that were influential in the development of 1960s counterculture in the United Kingdom. He later exhibited as "Boyle Family" with his partner and their two children. He spoke these words in a 1972 lecture at Newcastle University.

→ p. 39
BERTOLT BRECHT (1898–1956), a German dramatist and poet, won recognition after World War I for plays that pushed the boundaries of theater. When this line from the poem "Praise of Learning" was written, the Nazis, who later burned Brecht's work and drove him out of Germany, were on the rise.

→ p. 95
TANIA BRUGUERA (1968–) is a Cuban performance artist who has been arrested for work that challenges her government's suppression of political freedoms. These words are part of her answer to the question, "How important is art as a form of protest?" published in *Frieze* magazine in 2017.

→ p. 151
PEARL S. BUCK (1892–1973), an American author known for her novel *The Good Earth* (1931), won the Nobel Prize in Literature in 1938. A humanitarian and cofounder of the first international interracial adoption agency, Buck expressed this idea in her 1954 autobiography *My Several Worlds*.

→ p. 156
EDMUND BURKE (1729–1797) was an Irish statesman who served in the British Parliament for twenty-nine years. He is best known for his political writings, most notably his 1790 tract *Reflections on the Revolution in France*, a founding text of modern conservatism. These words come from a 1777 letter addressing American independence.

→ p. 48
ALBERT CAMUS (1913–1960) was a Nobel Prize–winning French Algerian author, philosopher, and journalist. In 1943, during his involvement in the French Resistance, he wrote the first of four wartime letters, quoted here, denouncing his friend's espousal of Nazism. They were later published together as *Letters to a German Friend*.

→ p. 70
RACHEL CARSON (1907–1964), an American marine biologist, wrote lyrical books on nature, including *Silent Spring* (1962), a best seller that awakened the public to the dangers of pollution and gave momentum to the global environmental movement. This statement is excerpted from a 1958 letter to her friend Dorothy Freeman, included in the 1994 collection *Always, Rachel*.

→ p. 38
CESAR CHAVEZ (1927–1993), a Mexican American activist whose family became migrant laborers during the Great Depression, founded a farm workers' union that achieved success via confrontational, nonviolent methods. These words are from a 1984 speech to the Commonwealth Club of San Francisco.

→ p. 139
WINSTON CHURCHILL (1874–1965) had a talent for oratory and diplomatic elegance that cemented his legacy as Britain's great wartime prime minister. He spoke these words, from one of his many powerful speeches, in 1941 to the boys of Harrow School, London, in the midst of World War II.

→ p. 68
LUCILLE CLIFTON (1936–2010) was a National Book Award–winning American poet who often wrote about her experiences as a black woman with rich, emotional depth. She expressed the belief quoted here in a 2007 *Mosaic* magazine interview.

→ p. 76
ANGELA DAVIS (1944–) is a leading American academic in feminist studies, critical race theory, and the history of consciousness. As one of the most public faces of the prison abolition movement, she has written extensively on the topic, including the 2016 book *Freedom Is a Constant Struggle*, from which these words are excerpted.

→ p. 142
DOROTHY DAY (1897–1980) was a journalist who in 1933 cofounded the *Catholic Worker*, a newspaper that promoted Catholic principles in fighting for social justice. Here she explains her goal, quoted by Studs Terkel in the introduction to his oral history collection *Hope Dies Last* (2003).

→ p. 131
JESSIE DE LA CRUZ (1919–2013) was a California native who began working at age five picking fruit and became a prominent organizer of farm workers and an activist for many causes. This statement lent the title to oral historian Studs Terkel's book *Hope Dies Last* (2003), in which it appears.

→ pp. 128–29
JEREMY DELLER (1966–), a London native, has won acclaim as a conceptual artist whose works often engage political concerns and invite public participation. His view on creativity as a force for change comes from *Frieze* magazine's 2017 piece "How Important Is Art as a Form of Protest?"

→ pp. 98–99
BHAIRAVI DESAI (1973–), who immigrated to New Jersey with her family from India as a child, helped found the New York Taxi Workers Alliance in response to the threat of restrictive regulations. Her words here were published in a 2011 *New Yorker* profile.

→ p. 145
JUNOT DÍAZ (1968–), a Dominican American writer, won the Pulitzer Prize for his 2007 novel *The Brief Wondrous Life of Oscar Wao*. This line appears in his short story "Otravida, Otravez," from the 2012 collection *This Is How You Lose Her*.

→ p. 53
FREDERICK DOUGLASS (1818–1895) escaped slavery and became a leader of the abolitionist movement in the United States. He made this observation in an 1857 speech marking the twenty-third anniversary of the abolition of slavery in the British West Indies and urging American abolitionists to keep up the struggle.

→ p. 106
LENA DUNHAM (1986–), a New York native, gained renown for creating and starring in the TV series *Girls*, which won praise for its honest portrayal of young women's lives. In the 2017 *New York Times* piece quoted here, "Harvey Weinstein and the Silence of the Men," Dunham urges all of us to speak out against sexual harassment and assault.

→ p. 174
SHIRIN EBADI (1947–), one of the first female judges in Iran, was forced to step down after the Iranian Revolution in 1979 and later became a lawyer for political dissidents. Winner of the 2003 Nobel Peace Prize for her defense of human rights, Ebadi offers these sage words in a 2017 *Guardian* profile.

→ p. 109
BARBARA EHRENREICH (1941–) is an author and activist whose work documents class and gender inequalities in the United States, as in her best-selling book *Nickel and Dimed* (2001). The words included here are from "Family Values," an essay in her collection *The Worst Years of Our Lives* (1990).

→ p. 44
ALBERT EINSTEIN (1879–1955), born in Germany, revolutionized physics with theories that opened dimensions beyond Isaac Newton's laws. He wrote these words in a 1931 letter to an Italian government minister urging him not to enact a plan requiring scientists to conduct their research in service of the fascist government. Einstein moved to the United States in 1933, when Hitler came to power.

→ p. 108
RALPH WALDO EMERSON (1803–1882), a Unitarian minister in Boston, left the church to pursue a more personal spirituality and helped launch the intellectual movement known as Transcendentalism. This line, from the essay "History" (1841), reminds readers that events of global significance stem from and are reflected in the knowledge and actions of individuals.

→ p. 111
MARTÍN ESPADA (1957–), a Brooklyn-born, award-winning poet and writer, has also worked as a housing lawyer defending tenants' rights. Here, in a 2001 interview reprinted in *Fire and Ink: An Anthology of Social Action Writing* (2009), he explains what keeps him engaged in making change.

→ p. 134
MICHEL FOUCAULT (1926–1984), a French philosopher, was arguably the most influential critical theorist of the postwar period, and his work on power and control in modern society remains indispensable to cultural and political thought. Foucault's belief stated here comes from a 1980 interview conducted at the University of California, Berkeley.

→ pp. 146–47
ANNE FRANK (1929–1945), born in Germany to a Jewish family, kept a diary during her two years in hiding from the Nazis in Amsterdam. Published in 1947, two years after her death at the Bergen-Belsen concentration camp, *The Diary of a Young Girl*, quoted here, made Frank an inspirational voice in the aftermath of the Holocaust.

→ p. 25
MAHATMA GANDHI (1869–1948), a London-trained barrister, pioneered nonviolent civil disobedience, first in a campaign for Indians' rights in South Africa and later in his native India, where he led the country's independence movement. This statement comes from a 1920 article published in his periodical, *Young India*.

→ p. 126
THEASTER GATES (1973–), a Chicago native, makes politically charged art that advances a hopeful vision of life, as in his *Dorchester Projects*, derelict houses he restores and turns into repositories of cultural inspiration. He is quoted here speaking about the *Dorchester Projects* in a 2015 *Observer* profile.

→ p. 157
NIKKI GIOVANNI (1943–), an American poet, rose to fame with her first poetry collection, *Black Feeling, Black Talk* (1967), which conveys the importance of developing black solidarity and awareness. This quotation, from a 1985 interview, expresses her belief in the power of continued protest and dissent.

→ p. 37
MIKHAIL GORBACHEV (1931–), the last leader of the Soviet Union, instituted reforms that ultimately led to the collapse of the USSR in 1991. He gave the speech quoted here at Stanford University in 1990, shortly after he was elected president and the same year he won the Nobel Peace Prize.

→ p. 58
SUSAN GRIFFIN (1943–) is an American feminist philosopher, essayist, and playwright whose genre-bending writings explore the interconnectedness of sexism, racism, and the effects of climate change. This encouragement is quoted in the foreword to the third edition of Rebecca Solnit's *Hope in the Dark* (2016).

→ pp. 132–33
DAG HAMMARSKJÖLD (1905–1961), son of a Swedish prime minister, served as secretary general of the United Nations from 1953 until his death in a plane crash that many suspect was plotted by his enemies. Hammarskjöld's advice quoted here comes from *Markings* (1963), a posthumously published journal.

→ p. 86
VÁCLAV HAVEL (1936–2011) was a noted Czech playwright, statesman, and political activist who led protests that brought about the 1989 Velvet Revolution overthrowing the ruling Communist Party. He reflects on becoming president of a democratic Czechoslovakia in this excerpt from his 2007 memoir, *To the Castle and Back*.

→ p. 33
HARRY HAY (1912–2002) was an American activist who is often remembered as the father of gay liberation. Hay believed in the importance of preserving minority identities and rejected the assimilationist strategies of the mainstream gay rights movement. His words here come from a 1998 interview with the magazine *The Progressive*.

→ p. 123
LILLIAN HELLMAN (1905–1984) was an American playwright perhaps best known for *The Little Foxes* (1939). When called to testify in 1952 before the House Un-American Activities Committee, she stated in the letter quoted here that she would refuse if the committee required her to implicate others and was blacklisted as a result.

→ p. 24
ABRAHAM JOSHUA HESCHEL (1907–1972), a Poland-born Jewish theologian who escaped the Holocaust and fled to the United States, wrote several influential books on Jewish spirituality and modeled his principles in his commitment to social activism. He wrote these words in a 1963 telegram to President John F. Kennedy accepting an invitation to discuss civil rights.

→ pp. 64–65
JENNY HOLZER (1950–) is an American text-based artist whose work, often installed in public spaces on a monumental scale, grapples with the power and implications of language. This text appears in a work from her *Survival Series* (1983–85), which explores realities of everyday life in contemporary society.

→ p. 32
ROBERT G. INGERSOLL (1833–1899), a celebrated orator, lawyer, and Civil War veteran, was a tireless advocate for the rights of women and African Americans. He spoke these words in an 1883 speech decrying the Supreme Court's decision to strike down the Civil Rights Act of 1875.

→ p. 117
THOMAS JEFFERSON (1743–1826) was the primary author of the Declaration of Independence and a proponent of individual liberty who started out as a Virginia lawyer and became the third president of the United States. The view expressed here comes from a 1787 letter to his like-minded friend James Madison.

→ p. 107
OWEN JONES (1984–), a British writer, activist, and columnist for the *Guardian*, addresses issues of class inequity. These words pointing to the current insidious trend toward corporate welfare are from his 2014 book *The Establishment: And How They Get Away with It*.

→ p. 127
JR (1983–), an urban activist, is a French artist known for his large-scale public photography projects that address questions of identity and agency in the age of globalization. His artistic mission to provoke change is encapsulated in this quotation, which is also the title of his 2011 TED Talk.

→ p. 159
JOHN F. KENNEDY (1917–1963), a World War II navy veteran, served in the House of Representatives and the Senate before being elected president in 1960. These words are from his 1962 speech commemorating the anniversary of the Alliance for Progress, his plan to promote economic development in Latin America.

→ p. 162
ROBERT F. KENNEDY (1925–1968), attorney general in his brother John F. Kennedy's presidential administration, regularly intervened to help campaigners for civil rights. Elected senator in 1964, he spoke these words on a visit to the University of Cape Town in 1966, in what is remembered as his Day of Affirmation Address.

→ p. 149
CORETTA SCOTT KING (1927–2006), wife of Martin Luther King Jr., was herself a tireless civil rights activist who devoted her life to positive social change. She expressed this opinion in a commencement address at Harvard University, delivered in her husband's stead, shortly after his 1968 assassination.

→ p. 31
MARTIN LUTHER KING JR. (1929–1968) was a Baptist minister who led the civil rights movement against racial inequality. He won the 1964 Nobel Peace Prize for powerful words and nonviolent protests that frequently cost him his freedom. He wrote the famous 1963 "Letter from Birmingham Jail," quoted here, to explain his actions to disapproving white clergy.

→ p. 75
NAOMI KLEIN (1970–) is a Canadian journalist whose first book No Logo (1999) examines the consequences of corporate branding and influence in the age of globalization. More recently she has focused on climate activism, with her 2014 best seller This Changes Everything, and frequently writes about current events. These words are excerpted from a 2003 Guardian piece on Argentina's presidential race.

→ p. 161
LARRY KRAMER (1935–), an American LGBT activist, public health advocate, and award-winning playwright, was instrumental in founding the influential AIDS Coalition to Unleash Power (ACT UP) in 1987. Kramer continues to promote awareness of the disease, as evidenced in these words from a 2003 New York Times article, "The Plague We Can't Escape."

→ pp. 136–37
BARBARA KRUGER (1945–), an American artist, began her career as a graphic designer before devoting herself to a multimedia practice. She offered this observation in a 2014 interview on the syndicated radio program The Dinner Party Download.

→ p. 158
JOHN LENNON (1940–1980) was a member of the epoch-making British band the Beatles. In this December 1969 Radio Luxembourg interview, Lennon explained how he hoped to sway public opinion against the Vietnam War with songs like "Give Peace a Chance" and gestures such as his "bed-ins" with his new wife, Yoko Ono.

→ p. 164
PRIMO LEVI (1919–1987), sent to Auschwitz from his native Italy in 1944, survived and in 1947 wrote the first of many celebrated books, If This Is a Man, which recounts his experiences in the Nazi concentration camp. His view on the necessity of remembering, expressed here, appears in his 1986 essay collection The Drowned and the Saved.

→ pp. 26–27
JOHN LEWIS (1940–) served as chairman of the Student Nonviolent Coordinating Committee (SNCC) from 1963 to 1966, becoming one of the most important leaders of the civil rights movement. A US congressman since 1987, Lewis continues to devote himself to social activism, as evidenced by this statement from the civil rights era he posted on Twitter.

→ p. 46
ABRAHAM LINCOLN (1809–1865), sixteenth president of the United States, spoke these words to a crowd in Bloomington, Illinois, on May 29, 1856. Part of an address that came to be known as his "Lost Speech," it was a condemnation of slavery so compelling that it was said reporters failed to take notes. A transcript (contested by some) was published in an 1896 issue of McClure's Magazine.

→ pp. 124–25
KEN LOACH (1936–) has made award-winning films that counter Hollywood fantasies with realistic portrayals of British class struggle, from *Kes* (1969) to his 2016 film, *I, Daniel Blake*. In a 2017 *Vox* interview, Loach offered this encouragement to artists working in the current hostile cultural climate.

→ p. 88
AUDRE LORDE (1934–1992), the daughter of West Indian immigrants, was an award-winning poet whose work spoke candidly about her experiences as a black lesbian in America. This statement from her 1977 speech "The Transformation of Silence into Language and Action" urged listeners to conquer fear and speak out in truth.

→ p. 101
ROSA LUXEMBURG (1871–1919), a Polish German revolutionary, split from the German Social Democratic Party (SPD) at the start of World War I to cofound the staunchly antiwar Spartacus League. These words are excerpted from an article published in November 1918, months before she was murdered by right-wing paramilitaries.

→ p. 50
WANGARI MAATHAI (1940–2011), a Kenyan veterinary anatomy professor, founded the Green Belt Movement in 1977, enlisting women to plant millions of trees. Maathai went on to become a government minister and in 2004 won the Nobel Peace Prize. Quoted here is her 2008 *Guardian* essay advising Kenya's warring factions on strategies for peace.

→ p. 144
EDDIE MABO (1936–1992), an indigenous Australian, fought a historic, ten-year-long court case that was finally won in 1992, five months after his death, legalizing indigenous peoples' rights to their ancestral land. Mabo's thoughts included here come from the 1996 book *Edward Koiki Mabo: His Life and Struggle for Land Rights*.

→ p. 150
ARCHIBALD MACLEISH (1892–1982) was an American modernist poet and playwright, three-time Pulitzer Prize winner, professor of rhetoric and oratory at Harvard, and ninth Librarian of Congress. Reflecting on the legacy of America's founding ideals, MacLeish wrote these words in a *New York Times* article published on the eve of the country's bicentennial in 1976.

→ p. 17
MALCOLM X (1925–1965), born Malcolm Little, changed his name when he joined the Nation of Islam in prison. As the organization's primary spokesperson, he powerfully influenced the civil rights movement, and the posthumously published *Autobiography of Malcolm X* (1965), from which this book's title comes, continues to inspire.

→ pp. 166–67
NELSON MANDELA (1918–2013), a lawyer and activist, was sentenced to life imprisonment in 1964 for fighting South Africa's apartheid system but was released in 1990. He became the country's first black president in 1994. Mandela spoke these words in 2005 at the 46664 Concert, an AIDS charity event held in Tromsø, Norway.

→ p. 30
THURGOOD MARSHALL (1908–1993) made his name as an attorney who argued critical civil rights cases, including the famous 1954 Supreme Court case *Brown v. Board of Education* mandating desegregation in public schools in America. Marshall became the first African American Supreme Court justice in 1967. His views here come from an archival television interview that has been frequently rebroadcast.

→ p. 120
IAN MCEWAN (1948–) is an English novelist whose critically acclaimed books include *Atonement* (2001) and the Booker Prize–winning *Amsterdam* (1998). The belief expressed here is excerpted from his 2015 commencement address at Dickinson College.

→ p. 47
BILL McKIBBEN (1960–), an American environmentalist, alerted a wide audience to the climate change crisis with his 1989 book *The End of Nature*, and he continues to spur grassroots action via his organization 350.org. He is quoted here in a *New Yorker* interview ahead of the 2014 People's Climate March, which he spearheaded.

→ p. 59
MARGARET MEAD (1901–1978) was an American anthropologist whose books, including *Coming of Age in Samoa* (1928), opened readers' eyes to cultural differences and who pursued causes ranging from women's rights to nuclear disarmament. With these words, excerpted from a 1976 *New York Times* piece, she warns voters of the dangers of political apathy.

→ pp. 60–61
HARVEY MILK (1930–1978), elected to San Francisco's board of supervisors in 1977, was a bold proponent of gay rights and one of the first openly gay elected officials in the United States. This excerpt is from a 1977 *Bay Area Reporter* interview.

→ p. 175
JOHN MILTON (1608–1674) expounded a worldview that emphasized human freedom and civil liberty, not only in such writings as the epic poem *Paradise Lost* (1667) but also in his capacity as a public servant during Britain's brief Commonwealth. Quoted here is his famous 1644 tract on free speech, the *Areopagitica*.

→ p. 89
GEORGE MONBIOT (1963–) is a British writer and activist who has traveled the world to highlight the damage inflicted on communities and the environment by unchecked capitalism. In the 2017 *Guardian* column quoted here, "Goodbye—and Good Riddance—to Livestock Farming," he urges readers to give up meat.

→ p. 62
TONI MORRISON (1931–), winner of the 1988 Pulitzer Prize for her novel *Beloved* and recipient of the 1993 Nobel Prize in Literature, reflects on and interrogates the afterlife of slavery in the United States. She also writes frequently on contemporary politics and culture, as in this 2015 article from the *Nation*.

→ p. 19
EDWARD R. MURROW (1908–1965) was a CBS radio correspondent who faithfully reported on key events during World War II. Rising to become one of America's most admired broadcast journalists, he issued this reminder in 1954 on his TV program *See It Now* as a challenge to Senator Joseph McCarthy's ruthless attempts to quash "communist" enemies.

→ p. 170
PABLO NERUDA (1904–1973), born Neftalí Ricardo Reyes Basoalto, wrote poetry during a career as a Chilean diplomat and politician. Quoted here is his 1971 speech accepting the Nobel Prize in Literature, for poetry that "brings alive a continent's destiny and dreams."

→ p. 115
REINHOLD NIEBUHR (1892–1971) was an American theologian who urged political engagement, especially against the rise of fascism and capitalist excess. These words come from his 1944 treatise on democracy and its preservation, *The Children of Light and the Children of Darkness*.

→ pp. 84–85
ANAÏS NIN (1903–1977) was a prolific French writer, known mostly for her lyrical diaries describing her bohemian life and loves in Paris and the United States. She made this observation in an entry from volume 3 of her published diaries (1939–44).

→ p. 63
BARACK OBAMA (1961–), a senator, lawyer, author, and former community organizer, was elected the United States' first African American president on a wave of optimism, stoked by his gift for oratory. These words come from a speech he made in Chicago on February 5, 2008, during the Democratic primaries.

→ pp. 140–41
GEORGE ORWELL (1903–1950), born to a British family in India, rejected his middle-class upbringing and began to write novels and nonfiction works with a strong social conscience, including *Nineteen Eighty-Four* (1949). This quotation is from a 1943 review of his friend Mulk Raj Anand's book *Letters on India*.

→ pp. 102–3
CAMILLE PAGLIA (1947–), an American academic and writer of *Sexual Personae* (1990) and other books, explodes political clichés and embraces Western cultural history in a way that leaves room for both tradition and personal freedom. The view expressed here is excerpted from a 2015 interview in the online magazine *Spiked Review*.

→ pp. 172–73
THOMAS PAINE (1737–1809) moved to the American colonies in 1774, when hostilities with his native England were escalating rapidly. In January 1776 he published the influential political pamphlet *Common Sense*, quoted here, which calls on American colonists to write a constitution for their own ideal republic.

→ p. 22
CHRISTABEL PANKHURST (1880–1958) was a British lawyer who, as a woman, was unable to practice. She led her suffragist mother, Emmeline, and sister, Sylvia, toward greater militancy in pursuing women's right to vote. In this 1908 speech, Pankhurst explains the need to "bring pressure to bear on the government."

→ p. 160
EMMELINE PANKHURST (1858–1928) devoted much of her life to fighting for women's right to vote in Britain, joining with her daughters to use increasingly militant tactics that more than once resulted in imprisonment. This explanation of the Pankhursts' stance comes from Emmeline's 1914 autobiography, *My Own Story*.

→ p. 52
ROSA PARKS (1913–2005) was an NAACP secretary from Alabama who in 1955 famously refused to give up her seat to a white man on a segregated bus. Parks recounted that historic moment in her 1992 autobiography *Rosa Parks: My Story*, excerpted here.

→ p. 74
PIER PAOLO PASOLINI (1922–1975) gained notoriety in his native Italy for his experimental, idiosyncratic films, including *Accattone* (1961), *Teorema* (1968), and *Salò, or the 120 Days of Sodom* (1975). He was also a prolific poet; this quote comes from "A Light," the appendix to his poem "The Religion of My Time" (1961).

→ p. 153
OCTAVIO PAZ (1914–1998), a Nobel Prize–winning Mexican author and diplomat, brought great independence of thought to his poetry and prose. He made this observation while recounting a memory of his mother in a 1995 *Los Angeles Times* interview.

→ p. 135
MARIA POPOVA (1984–) was born in Bulgaria and now resides in New York. In 2006 she started her influential blog *Brain Pickings*, an encyclopedic survey of, as she puts it, "what matters in the world and why." In the 2015 post quoted here, "Hope, Cynicism, and the Stories We Tell Ourselves," she rejects media-influenced negativity.

→ p. 112
DIEGO RIVERA (1886–1957) was criticized by the press for the perceived "anticapitalist" message of murals he painted at the Detroit Institute of Arts in 1933. In a lecture given the same year at the New Workers' School in New York, excerpted here, the Mexican artist addressed the controversy and urged artists to consider their potential as agents of progress.

→ p. 87
PAUL ROBESON (1898–1976), an American actor, singer, and key figure of the Harlem Renaissance, was driven to political activism by the rise of Francisco Franco's fascist dictatorship and the outbreak of the Spanish Civil War. His belief quoted here comes from a 1937 speech delivered at a rally for Spanish war refugees.

→ p. 94
ELEANOR ROOSEVELT (1884–1962), First Lady for twelve years, was an outspoken social activist and diplomat who in 1948 oversaw the drafting of the UN's Universal Declaration of Human Rights. This is a line from her last book, *Tomorrow Is Now* (1963), written on her deathbed at age seventy-eight.

→ p. 169
FRANKLIN D. ROOSEVELT (1882–1945), the longest-serving president in US history, led the country's economic recovery from the Great Depression with ambitious social welfare legislation known as the New Deal. In the 1940 speech quoted here, Roosevelt promised full US material support for Allied forces in World War II.

→ p. 154
THEODORE ROOSEVELT (1858–1919), elected vice president to William McKinley in 1900, assumed the presidency after McKinley's assassination in 1901. The speech quoted here was his first address to Congress, given in December of that year.

→ p. 130
ARUNDHATI ROY (1961–), whose 1997 Booker Prize–winning first novel *The God of Small Things* made her famous far beyond her hometown of Delhi, has since written mainly nonfiction, seeking to combat the catastrophic effects of globalization. In "Confronting Empire," the 2003 speech quoted here, she describes a hopeful vision of the future.

→ p. 171
SALMAN RUSHDIE (1947–), a British Indian writer and winner of the Booker Prize for *Midnight's Children* (1981), found himself the target of a fatwa ordered by Iranian leader Ayatollah Khomeini for his depiction of Islam in *The Satanic Verses* (1988). He spoke these words in his 2015 commencement address at Emory University.

→ p. 168
BERTRAND RUSSELL (1872–1970), a British philosopher and Nobel Prize–winning author, was also a lifelong activist, twice imprisoned as an antiwar agitator. In the 1951 *New York Times* piece quoted here, "No Funk, No Frivolity, No Fanaticism," he urges resilience in the face of Cold War anxieties.

→ p. 138
BAYARD RUSTIN (1912–1987), chief organizer of the 1963 March on Washington, remained an activist throughout his life with his efforts toward racial integration, workers' rights, and gay rights. These words urging active participation are from his 1970 commencement address at the Tuskegee Institute in Alabama.

→ p. 49
RUBY SALES (1948–) made news as an American teenage civil rights activist when she testified against a man who had shot at her, killing a white protester instead. She went on to become a public theologian seeking to build communities based on "right relations" and is quoted here in a 2016 episode of the radio program *On Being*.

→ p. 69
GEORGE SANTAYANA (1863–1952), was a Spanish American philosopher who wrote eloquent, influential books about the nature of existence and human intelligence. This well-known statement is taken from his monumental five-volume work *The Life of Reason* (1905–6).

→ p. 143
GEORGE SAUNDERS (1958–), a Texas native trained as a geophysicist, found his true calling as a keen observer of contemporary America whose fiction has won awards including the Booker Prize. A professor at Syracuse University, he included this advice in a 2013 convocation speech to graduating seniors.

→ p. 54
THEODORE SHAW (1954–), a law professor at the University of North Carolina and former NAACP counsel, has litigated civil rights cases from trial level to the Supreme Court involving such issues as police misconduct, housing, and employment. This statement comes from Studs Terkel's oral history *Hope Dies Last* (2003).

→ pp. 78–79
ELLEN JOHNSON SIRLEAF (1938–) served as the twenty-fourth president of Liberia from 2006–2018, the first elected female head of state in Africa. She spoke these words at Harvard University, her alma mater, in 2011, the same year that she shared a Nobel Peace Prize for her efforts to uphold women's rights.

→ p. 100
REBECCA SOLNIT (1961–) is an American writer perhaps best known for her 2008 essay "Men Explain Things to Me," which articulated the concept of "mansplaining." The observation quoted here comes from her 2004 book *Hope in the Dark*, about the need for idealism and the effectiveness of taking part in change.

→ p. 122
SUSAN SONTAG (1933–2004) was a prolific American writer whose essay collections are landmarks of contemporary cultural criticism. Excerpted here is "On Courage and Resistance," a speech she gave at a 2003 ceremony for the Óscar Romero Award honoring human rights advocates.

→ p. 66
ELIZABETH CADY STANTON (1815–1902), daughter of a New York congressman, was determined to fight laws that discriminated against women and, with Susan B. Anthony, led the women's suffrage movement in the United States. In her 1892 speech "The Solitude of Self," quoted here, she argued that equal rights are essential "for the complete development of every individual."

→ p. 155
GLORIA STEINEM (1934–), an American journalist and activist, launched the feminist magazine *Ms.* in 1972. Steinem has tirelessly promoted women's equality, and she has stated that the idea quoted here, published on her website, is "the shortest way I've been able to write my beliefs."

→ p. 97
SARAH SZE (1969–), an American sculptor, installation artist, and recipient of a 2003 MacArthur "Genius Grant," frequently comments in her work on the proliferation of information and material objects in contemporary life. These words appeared in the catalogue for *Protest*, a 2016 exhibition at Victoria Miro gallery in London.

→ p. 77
STUDS TERKEL (1912–2008), a Chicago radio host, interviewed ordinary people on his show *The Studs Terkel Program*, which began airing in 1952. He soon turned to creating award-winning books compiling the honest views of fellow citizens. This line from the introduction of his 2003 book *Hope Dies Last* summarizes his take on the source of social change.

→ p. 121
HENRY DAVID THOREAU (1817–1862) was an American writer who is best remembered for *Walden* (1854), his account of a spiritual life in nature. Thoreau's 1849 essay "Civil Disobedience," quoted here, defends his refusal to obey an unjust government that upheld slavery. It was an inspiration to civil rights leaders in the 1960s.

→ p. 113
NADYA TOLOKONNIKOVA (1989–), a member of the Russian feminist-punk group Pussy Riot, was arrested in 2012 along with her bandmates for their controversial performance in a Moscow church protesting President Vladimir Putin's reelection. While incarcerated she began a correspondence with the philosopher Slavoj Žižek, from which this statement is excerpted.

→ p. 20
LEO TOLSTOY (1828–1910), was a Russian author best known for his novels *War and Peace* (1869) and *Anna Karenina* (1878). His writing often grappled with issues of social justice, stressing the impact of ordinary individuals' moral conduct in shaping history, as in this line from the 1900 pamphlet *Some Social Remedies*.

→ p. 23
SOJOURNER TRUTH (ca. 1797–1883) was born into slavery and escaped to freedom in 1826, becoming a revolutionary figure in the abolitionist and women's rights movements. This impassioned statement comes from a speech at an American Equal Rights Association meeting in 1867 in which she urged consideration of black women's rights in the women's suffrage movement.

→ p. 36
DESMOND TUTU (1931–), a South African Anglican cleric, faced death threats in promoting the anti-apartheid movement, but his eloquent advocacy and nonviolent tactics saw him awarded the Nobel Peace Prize in 1984. These words, spoken in a 1999 TV interview with journalist Bill Moyers, sum up his apartheid-era message.

→ pp. 118–19
MARK TWAIN (1835–1910), an American writer born Samuel Clemens, adopted his pen name to author such classic works as *Adventures of Huckleberry Finn* (1884). Twain's unpretentious wisdom comes through in these words from a journal he kept in the years 1887 and 1888.

→ p. 51
LECH WAŁĘSA (1943–), an electrician who led Poland's trade union, Solidarity, won concessions from the communist government but was frequently detained. Awarded the 1983 Nobel Peace Prize, Wałęsa expressed in his Nobel lecture, excerpted here, the determination that helped hasten the collapse of Soviet rule. In 1990 he became the president of Poland.

→ pp. 82–83
DAVID FOSTER WALLACE (1962–2008) established himself as one of America's preeminent writers with his sprawling, satirical novel *Infinite Jest* (1996). This observation appears in "Up, Simba," a piece he wrote for *Rolling Stone* about John McCain's 2000 presidential primary campaign.

→ pp. 92–93
ANDY WARHOL (1928–1987), an American artist and cult figure, was known almost as well for his pithy insights as for his iconic paintings of Campbell's Soup cans. This observation is from his 1975 book *The Philosophy of Andy Warhol*.

→ p. 90
ROB WATSON (1961–), an American environmental scientist who led the formulation of the LEED green rating system for buildings, has worked to move the construction industry toward sustainable practices. His friend, the *New York Times* columnist Thomas Friedman, included this quotation in his 2010 editorial "We're Gonna Be Sorry."

→ p. 80
<u>SIMONE WEIL</u> (1909–1943), a French philosopher, mystic, and teacher, devoted herself to political activism at an early age and continued to fight for the rights of laborers throughout her life. These galvanizing words are excerpted from a notebook she kept between the years 1933 and 1939.

→ p. 43
<u>IDA B. WELLS</u> (1862–1931), born into slavery, was an American journalist who used her voice to draw national attention to lynchings of black men across the South. This statement is from her pamphlet *Southern Horrors: Lynch Law in All Its Phases*. After its publication in 1892, persistent threats forced her to leave her home in Memphis.

→ p. 114
<u>CORNEL WEST</u> (1953–), a Harvard University philosophy professor, is also an activist and author of such books as the influential *Race Matters* (1993), in which he speaks to America's complex struggles with race. These words are included in a 2009 talk titled "Cornel West's Catastrophic Love," posted on the website BigThink.com.

→ p. 72
<u>WALT WHITMAN</u> (1819–1892) revolutionized American poetry with his collection *Leaves of Grass*, originally published in 1855 and revised throughout his life. He is also known for his nonfiction work, including *Democratic Vistas* (1871), excerpted here, a critique of American democracy in the aftermath of the Civil War.

→ p. 81
<u>ELIE WIESEL</u> (1928–2016), born in Romania, survived the Holocaust and became an American human rights activist who authored numerous books recounting his harrowing experiences in Auschwitz and Buchenwald. He shared this urgent directive in his acceptance speech for the Nobel Peace Prize in 1986.

→ p. 96
<u>ELLA WHEELER WILCOX</u> (1850–1919) was an American poet whose work won a popular following for its expressions of optimism and hope. This line comes from "Protest," published in her 1914 collection *Poems of Problems*.

→ p. 116
<u>OSCAR WILDE</u> (1854–1900), born in Ireland, was a writer known for his outsize personality as well as his works, perhaps most famously *The Picture of Dorian Gray* (1890). In the essay quoted here, "The Soul of Man under Socialism" (1891), he expresses a typically paradoxical view of society.

→ p. 40
<u>VIRGINIA WOOLF</u> (1882–1941), a British writer, was a pioneer of modernist literature who experimented in her fiction with portraying the fleeting and fragmentary nature of consciousness. In the 1929 extended essay *A Room of One's Own*, from which these words are taken, she responds to society's strictures on women's freedom of expression.

→ pp. 104–5
<u>MALALA YOUSAFZAI</u> (1997–), born in Pakistan, gained international recognition at age eleven for her courageous blogging about life under Taliban rule and in 2012 survived an assassination attempt by the Taliban. She is a passionate advocate for equal access to education, and in 2014 was a corecipient of the Nobel Peace Prize. Her statements here are from a 2013 *Glamour* magazine profile.

Phaidon Press Limited
Regent's Wharf
All Saints Street
London N1 9PA

Phaidon Press Inc.
65 Bleecker Street
New York, NY 10012

phaidon.com

First published 2018
© 2018 Phaidon Press Limited

ISBN 978 0 7148 7673 3

A CIP catalog record for this book is
available from the British Library and the
Library of Congress.

Researcher and Project Editor: Sara Bader
Editorial Assistant: Simon Hunegs
Additional research and editing: Susan Welsh
Biographies: Susan Welsh and Simon Hunegs
Production Controller: Adela Cory
Design: Julia Hasting
Page layout: Julia Hasting and Elana Schlenker

Printed in Italy

FRONT MATTER SOURCES:

p. 6: Gloria Steinem, keynote address at
Women and Power conference, Omega Institute,
Rhinebeck, New York, September 11–13, 2009.

pp. 7–9: Jacey Fortin, "Republicans Tweet,
Then Delete, a Fake Lincoln Quote,"
New York Times, February 13, 2017.

p. 8: Zadie Smith, "That Crafty Feeling,"
in Changing My Mind: Occasional Essays
(New York: Penguin, 2009), 102.

p. 10: Michel de Montaigne, "Of the Education
of Children," in The Works of Michel de
Montaigne, trans. William Hazlitt
(Philadelphia: J. W. Moore, 1856), 86.

p. 12: Richard Ford, interview by Ben Pfeiffer,
Rumpus, November 26, 2014.

pp. 14–15: Geoffrey O'Brien, "We Are What
We Quote," Opinionator blog, New York Times,
March 2, 2013.